Flat White, C

Also by Libby Sommer and published by Ginninderra Press

My Year With Sammy
The Crystal Ballroom
The Usual Story
Stories from Bondi
Lost in Cooper Park
The Cellist, a Bellydancer & Other Distractions

Libby Sommer

Flat White, One Sugar

Illustrations by Natasha Sommer

With love to my children, my grandchildren,
and to their partners.

With gratitude to my mentor, editor
and dear friend Susanne Gervay OAM
and to the Wednesday Night Poets
for encouragement and editing advice,
and to Judith Rooney
for creative suggestions.

Flat White, One Sugar
ISBN 978 1 76109 690 7
Copyright © text Libby Sommer 2024
Front cover pastel drawing: Natasha Sommer
Internal illustrations: Natasha Sommer
Back cover photo: Jason Painter

First published 2024 by
Ginninderra Press
PO Box 3461 Port Adelaide 5015
www.ginninderrapress.com.au

Contents

It is necessary to write, if the days are not to slip emptily by. How else, indeed, to clap the net over the butterfly of the moment? For the moment passes, it is forgotten; the mood is gone; life itself is gone. That is where the writer scores over his fellows: he catches the changes of his mind on the hop.

– Vita Sackville-West

Foreword

Flat White, One Sugar is my second poetry collection. My first, *The Cellist, a Bellydancer & Other Distractions* (Ginninderra Press), was published in 2022.

Writing poetry is a way for me to explore the world around me and within me, to make sense of my experiences and emotions, and to connect with the universal human experience. It allows me to distil the complexities of life, to capture a moment in time, or a feeling that is difficult to express in any other way.

In this collection, the poems touch on a wide range of topics, from the beauty of nature to the difficulties of love, from the joys of childhood to the challenges of ageing.

I am very proud that my granddaughter, Natasha Sommer, a graduate of the National Art School, has illustrated *Flat White, One Sugar.*

Out and About

Poetry begins where language starts: in the shadows and
accidents of one person's life.
– Eaven Boland

Jogger At My Heels

Each morning he races up the steep
steps of the gully and then down again

on the path I take
to buy my daily newspaper.

I recognise his exhalations just behind
and apologetic grimace running back,

urging me to move aside
to let him through,

but today I understand him
more fully than before.

Hearing my own heavy breathing
as I walk up the gigantic slope

I'm sure he'd like to say, *Don't rush
don't rush.*

…but he's in too much of a hurry.

The Corner Café

Her ears pierced with studs & stones & circles of gold give
me great pleasure, standing opposite her to place my order.
That someone can design parallels and diagonals in the
grooves of their ear lobes, like vivid stars in a dark sky. She
wears eyeliner thick and black with an upward tick, her
eyebrows tattooed in perfect arches. Her eyes shine above her
mask as she agrees the air conditioner is just what we need on
days like this. She's walked to work in the heat. On her feet
all day on the front line, face to face giving service to others.
We would wither were it not for her radiance.

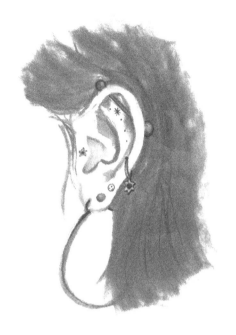

Words

Belly expansions and contractions,
turning our attention to sensations,
we remember the three things you said:
breathe light, breathe slow, breathe deep.

We take control. Above us
the air conditioner hums.
At your own pace, no need to rush.
Next door a conference
of 43 dentists learn
sensation management.
I swallow the urge to laugh.

A full exhale, let it all go.
Your words give comfort
as they enter the gaps
between in and out,
slowing down.
Everything will be just fine.

Afterwards, the morning looks different.
Good work everyone.
Well done.
We roll up our mats,
head for our cars –
safe from the pain,
for now.

Electioneering On the Mall

Actually, I know which party
I will *not* be voting for.

I am a true blue Australian
hammered by our land of droughts
and flooding rains.

When it's election
broadcast blackout time
I breathe a sigh of relief.

> What? Please move so I can get by.
> Yes, I know about early voting.
> No, you won't get me to
>
> swing a different way.

A Refuge

Do you know, St Honoré Bakery,
your large black & white floor tiles
show the exact space for Social Distancing?
Your blackboard menu out front
flags passage to the shopping centre.
Surely sophisticated French indulgences
upstage all else inside,
your gateaux worthy of any Parisian patisserie:
flaky puff pastry, velvety cream,
bite-sized choux balls.

But where are you on Sunday mornings, St Honoré,
when the early cyclists ride past?
Your door is closed, your ovens unlit.
Here come gumboots & wet umbrellas
as we all live through wild weather
– back-to-back La Niñas –
and teachers from across the road arrive
in shoes with stiletto heels.

Don't we all need a dry haven
from unrelenting winter storms?
East of the city, weather-eroded beaches
promise summer sunshine
for our light-deprived eyes.

As the ocean comes up to the land,
we hope these beaches don't disappear.
There's blue sky to wish for
in a gap in the clouds.
St Honoré, patron saint of bakers
& pastry cooks, I think I'm addicted to you.
I'm wondering, will your baking give
hope & warmth today?

Newspaper

A small gift arrives most days

waits patiently in the quiet corners

We open up to it

accept its offering

in the pauses between things

The older man

'here's my newspaper?' he said

because he saw a woman

sit alone in the café

Calculations

We exchanged Instagram handles:
this means we are friends,
that you followed me
and I followed you back.

Remember at the photo rally
our team of 7, a map, the list of 12 clues:
*expand your creativity & community
with photography.*

We cannot be judged, you & me,
age, after all, is just a number:
intergenerational relationships can work.
Let me tell you more of the places I love,

by the harbour, by the sea
then you tell how best to use the light,
shapes, angles, lines,

how many hours it takes to imagine
something that wasn't there before.

Tactics

A woman is hitting back & forth
across the net, a peaked cap
secured by her ponytail.
Can she overcome the self-doubt,
anxiety & lapses of concentration?
She mustn't let her mind
be the winner in this battle.
Right here, right now,
she's in control,
even in the wind,
alternating her drives
to the far corners of the court.
Nothing distracts her,
not the noisy leaf blower
or her male opponent
with superior physical strength.
Tactics are her best weapon.
Now she is serving,
tossing the ball high,
straight as an arrow,
reaching up,
accelerating,
out wide
to his left-handed backhand.
She ignores her cap
escaping with the wind
as she executes
a perfect follow through.
She smiles.
Ace! It's an ace.

Melody

Music expresses that which cannot be said and on which it is
impossible to be silent.
– Charles Darwin

Bodhran

It's been sleeping quietly at the back
of the cupboard for years.

I used to flick a tipper stick against
its goatskin head each day.
Neighbours tapped their feet to its
syncopated rhythms.

Tricky hand movements on
the inside ruled pitch & timbre –
jigs & reels or slow, slow
steady heartbeat.

I greased oil into its stretched skin.
My teachers, percussionists, turned feral
at music festivals *en plein air.*

Be brave now. Pick up the drum,
relax the shoulders,
loosen the grip –
but can I hear the patterns
like I used to then?

Rhythmic beats
in the lengthening shadows –
or are they footsteps
labouring up the stairs?

Not Easy

In the community hall at the wharf
a teacher with soprano ukulele

is strumming and singing to his class
of adult learners –
once I would have said elderly students
before I became ancient myself

his vocal skills diminished by a mask
uke chords and finger-picked notes
bouncing off brick walls and out the door
only four strings reverberating as if amplified
but lighter   dynamic patterns   carnival of sound
lighting up all four lobes of our brains
strengthening neural circuits
tapping our feet   *down down down-up down-up*
never saying   *I'm too old for imprinting*

out the window seagulls swoop and flap
above the young homeless man
asleep with his dog   guitar   skateboard   suitcases
I wonder what his story is –
will he pick up his guitar and sing?
beside him   *please help   we need blankets*
warm clothing   dog toys   dog food
people with dogs in woollen coats
jog past   not present   introverted buds
blocking us all out

the teacher scans the room
glad of an audience   *doesn't anyone want to sing?*

our knotted fingers contort and stretch
press down hard on wired frets
          you're doing well
you're all doing very well

Sound and Spaces

Some mornings
I get to hear
a symphony of birds
before the first train hisses
around the curve of the tunnel.
The rhythmic woo-woo of a koel
as dawn brightens the sky.
Sounds and then the gaps between.

The music is not in the notes,
but in the spaces
between them, Debussy wrote.

That's how I like to communicate.
Not *blab blab blab*.
Well, sometimes *blab*, but also pauses.
People like to chronicle something
and then hear what you think
of what they've just said.

Bless *Quiet Carriages!*
The soothing repetitive
clicks & clacks as the wheels
of the train beat time on the tracks.

There was a pigeon inspecting
the floor of the café this morning
scratching up crumbs between the tables,
a proud black pigeon, but when he strutted
up to the counter, he didn't utter a word –
just an intermittent *coo coo coo.*

The Uke Tuner

I don't recall where I bought this small
clip-on music tuner for strings.
Was it from one of my teachers
or from a now-nearly-non-existent music store?
I press its tiny buttons, again, again,
till I get to U for Ukulele,
then pluck each nylon string
until the little arm hits the right note
and its small square screen
lights up in luminous green.
G, then C, E then A.
Good Children Eat Apples.
That's how I remember the order of strings.
But where did I buy this useful device?
Like so many things, I have no recollection.
Sometimes I watch a person's name vanish as soon
as it is spoken, like the once-familiar melodies
plucked on the strings of this uke,
even the lyrics,
fading into yesterday.

Enmity

What passing bells for those who die as cattle?
Only the monstrous anger of the guns.
– Wilfred Owen

News Break

A blast of new horrors:
ceasefire broken in Mariupol,
steel works hiding civilians bombed.
We're watching loved ones
die excruciating deaths from injuries.
Scenes of bloody battle.
In Shanghai, people dragged
from their homes kicking & screaming
by health workers in hazmat suits
as the city's lockdown enters
its seventh week.
A person put in a body bag
in Beijing, while still alive.
Haversacks & hold-alls of anguish.
Can't watch. Can't listen.
Enough.
Enough already.

Holding On

When we are wet and cold,
we shelter under umbrellas & awnings.

When a lizard is wet and cold – often seeming
frozen or dead – they drop from trees, stunned.
They've shut down, no longer able to hold on.

It's true they like to wake up in the warm sun,
just like us, even though they are cold-blooded.
Maybe a blue-tongue lizard's easy-going nature
is what makes them a popular pet.
Maybe it's their striking blue tongue.

You see lizards climbing the brick facade
of your house as the rain keeps pelting down.
They may hibernate in a hole in the ground,
or maybe a tree trunk or a fallen log.
City living is challenging if you're
clinging to walls & windows. Scaling
a windowpane without falling off is one thing.

When enemies approach, some reptiles,
nicknamed *the Jesus Christ lizard*, can run on water.
If surprised by a predator, some lizards can detach
their tails or change colour to escape their enemies.
Others can look in two directions at once.

We're looking in the direction of human predators
executing genocide far away in a war.
We can't make it stop.
Is there nothing we can do?

To hang on, lizards have evolved
larger and stickier feet, while wild winds
blow your umbrella inside out. These reptiles
have come to grips with their changed lives.

Maybe we don't want to keep looking at
images of suffering. Rather, we could
get ourselves a *biodiversity conservation licence*
and keep an eye on a blue-tongue
backyard buddy,
or not.

Twisted Tea

I splattered the last of my favourite
loose leaf tea all over the floor today,
when I lost my grip on the lid.
Twisted Oolong produced in Ukraine
it said on the label.
But it is a time of such sadness,
a spilt canister of loose leaf
is hardly worth mentioning.
So many shattered tea sets
buried in the rubble.
Ceramic pots and porcelain mugs,
smashed.
Fierce railroads bombed, buildings, farms.
Civilians tortured.

'Filthy scumbags,'
said President Zelensky.
'What else can you call them?'

I watch a woman sob on camera.
'Their soldiers are barbaric.
They don't understand.
They are murderers.'

It is hard to consider sipping tea
without crying into the cup.
Will the small tea plantation
– out of the line of fire for now –
be spared?
I'm holding as tight as I can
to the thought that one day
we'll be able to celebrate
with a pot of rare twisted oolong loose
leaf tea produced on a small farm
tucked away somewhere
in a corner of Ukraine.

If Only Things Could Be Different

Two sets of kookaburras
Side by side
On my clothesline
Beaks down
Ready for attack
Two matching sets of snake & lizard
Dive-bomb killers

I didn't know at first the Kookaburra Totem
Teaches that a kookaburra's
Strong bold energy indicates
A time of signals and omens

I'd thought of kookaburras
As laughing querents – ones who seek
Predictors of rain
But that's all
Although I knew they roosted
In family groups snuggled up together
On solid branches

But while I watched a kookaburra
Hurtle downwards
It was another day that humans
Dropped bombs on innocent people

Lives cut short

Branches fallen from unstable trees.

Things I Wonder About

i)

Mountains masked by fog in the wet
as rain-soaked farmers wait for rivers to ebb.
Dawn, that lightener of darkness,
stands by – catcher of dreams?

ii)

The invasion continues.
On the other side of the world,
we imagine the screams
of drones and cruise missiles.
His only weapon left
is to brutalise individual
citizens – President Biden.

iii)

Two years of pandemic,
fear of war and
the energy crisis –

White cockatoos land
safely on the steel railing
one by one –

I want to live lightly as a bird in flight –

Walk waterproofed into the weeks of wet –

iv)

I wonder
how to know
what is the truth.
Lies of omission
are still
lies.

When Will It End?

The woman is weeping for her husband,
his ashes lined up with the unclaimed
urns at the crematorium.

How could this happen again?

The man is weeping for his dead wife
& unborn child stretchered out from
the bombed maternity hospital.

The woman says, 'We had to flee. His ashes
were left behind.'

What use is a city of rubble?

The brother is weeping beside his mother at the grave
of his twin. The brothers had strapped on fatigues,
taken up weapons, knowing they may die – sons,
brothers, husbands & fathers.

Each day the mind grapples: no power,
no water, starvation,

but Ukrainians, bigger than their fears,
face the Goliath. Church bells ring
calling the world to stand beside them.

Look at this man in body armour on the news
saying farewell to his wife and child.

Last week a teacher of children, today a soldier,
when will he see his school again?

Russia's War

Beginning their encirclement
said a retired major general.
They've *gained ground*
in their invasion.
Triumphalism has crept into narratives
he said discussing
the changing tides of fortune.
But the *brutal cauldron*
spread itself across the sky
armed with its lying narrative.
Another retired strategist warned,
long, bitter and destructive,
a phrase repeated often recently,
and *indescribably difficult,*
as each strove by physical force
to compel the other to submit to its will.
Force braced. Then escalated.
More death and brutality
than it had imagined. Both sides
willing, however, to continue.

Epiphany

Was not writing poetry a secret transaction,
a voice answering a voice?
– Virginia Woolf

Flat White, One Sugar

Up above is special to the birds.
A new craft beer is special to schooner-lovers,
who know it will have a unique aftertaste
before they've even had a sip.
The beanie warming the newborn
is special to the mum
swaddling her in hospital.
The cough is special, wretchedly, to the throat.
The wish you hold secretly inside yourself
is special to your being.
The gumboots are special to dry feet,
more special than the joggers,
which are special only in the gym.
The video of the runners
is not special to the owner of the phone
but is special to the competitors in the race.
I don't want to be special to baristas
who ask how was my weekend,
or people bent over hand-held devices,
not special to those who don't listen
when I answer their questions.
I want to be as special
as a morning coffee addiction,
but in the way a scarf is special,
or warm gloves,
not because they stand out from the crowd,
but because they know
they give comfort to others.

Re-entry

It was a hard trudge out from under the cloud.
She numbered off entire months
as she raised each foot,
remembering long nights dropping like thunder.
We just have to stumble on.
She sees the season changing
in the jasmine air, the swooping birds,
the vivid trees.
She welcomed these into her sacred spaces,
saved them on memory sticks for revisiting,
celebrated streets turned purple
with the delicate release of jacaranda blooms.
If she were to let loose in the world,
these are her re-entry points,
through these she learned
we've just got to move forward,
but how to do it, steadily as a bud
knowing when to open up its petals?

Transience

A luminous, tangerine, and blazing expanse
burst out to the left of the blue
from the harbour to the city as the western light
lowered itself behind concrete high-rises.
We watched from the hill,
took a seat on the park bench,
the lawn with its after-the-rain moistness
too wet to lie back on.
We knew we had to seize
this fleeting moment.

We were spectators of that sensational
display, after enduring the restrictions
that made us change and mutate,
shape-shifting during the months,
then the years, of the pandemic,
wearing us down, teaching us
adapt, adapt, adapt,
change, change, change.

Today we search for the brilliance
unfolding in the sky.

Mindfulness

1

The Master says,
Remember to sit in the seat
of centred awareness.
Don't fuse with
your thoughts –
they'll suck you in.
As long as you're watching,
you're not getting lost in them.

2

Sometimes cast-iron teapots
have lessons to teach us,
sitting steadily
beside small mugs on
a bamboo tray.
They are not looking back
at echoes from the past.

3

Bunch of native plants,
red-brushed, silver-leafed,
centred in a vase.
The early morning café
hisses and froths.
No other sound grabs me by the ear.

Beckoning

At dawn
a sense of hope infiltrates
my bedroom,

a thrum of trucks idling outside,
bins rolled, garbage spat out,

young seagulls crying for food
from their parents.

Even if I don't know what the birds
are signalling, their familiar
call & responses comfort me.

Down at the bay
a ferry sounds its horn.
A man with a bucket
and fishing rod
passes below my window.

Life is on the move
in the beckoning light.

What Could We Say?

Before dawn's soft lightening,
rain stills itself on flat roofs
in pools of stagnant water.

Each morning we hear
a car speed up the hill
and dark recurring dreams
which tossed and turned
our restless selves, leave us
twisted in the sheets.

Now we start
warming rooms,
opening blinds.

Into the silence,
tight with the unspoken,
our thoughts pokerfaced
– space enough not given or seized –

moments hang,
more half-empty
than half-full.

I Said To a Woman I Used To Know

How are you today?
Two weeks after the incident
we were lined up outside
the gym studio, waiting to go in.
What news?
But the eyes of the woman who used
to be my friend bore into my skull.
'News?' she jeered,
'Groundhog Day. You know what
that means, don't you?'
Then she turned her back to talk to
the person in front. My stomach knotted.
The gym smelt more disinfected than usual.
Antiseptic clean, but bleak.
Can sterile smell bleak?

Awake

My phone's clock face saying 3 a.m.
has become my loathed companion.

It wants to be a flash in the dark, the latest update.
It gets far too much of my attention.

Without numbers, the phone clock
is like a plant-based hamburger

unable to satisfy the meat-eater.
4 a.m., 5 a.m., 6 a.m.,

the hours struggle towards dawn.
Without numbers, I am the directionless wind,

too hesitant to blow the curtains
apart and begin the morning.

Familiarity

When they tell you they think
they've met you before, say you have
one of those familiar faces.
Your stomach may lurch;
you don't want to have one of those
familiar faces.

When they ask you to a house party,
hesitate before answering.
You don't like having one of those faces,
and you don't want to go.
What if their back door is locked
and you can't make a quick escape?
Someone may trap you with their long story,
especially when they say you could use it.
Tell them they should write it themselves.

If they say they will be in touch very soon,
just nod.

You don't want to spend time with them.
They want something from you
because of your familiar face.
You're safeguarding your energy
for something that needs serious reflection.
Your mother, your father, your brother as a boy.
Tell them you're working on a complex project
that will take forever.

Plan to open the front door again soon,
just a little, and see what's out there.
Remember to keep your eyelids up like a roller blind.
Know you could be snapped shut at any time.

Calamity

Poetry is thoughts that breathe, and words that burn.
– Thomas Gray

Snapped

The Thursday we meet up at the park
shockingly lets loose
a flash flood in New York, people trapped
in basement apartments. The recounting
of a suicide, same Thursday
my son decides to remarry.
Stabbing rampage in New Zealand
right before ABBA announces
a comeback after a four decades split.
Fifteen hundred species of fish
struggling to survive in the world's
largest reef system. You said again
books are your lifeline, on the same
Thursday you told me
she jumped out of the window
taking the baby with her.

Dangerous Liaisons

Lately I've felt you everywhere,
especially at dawn and dusk.

Some said N, N-Diethyl-meta-Toluamide
would stop you, that you'd
buzz off, like a toxic lover.

The sleeplessness of hot nights
carried the sound of your presence.

Last summer, after heavy rainfalls
followed by high temperatures,
M had taken me for a picnic in the park
where you flew around
before sucking our blood.
He'd wondered how you'd survived
the extreme drought, said you must
have been in diapause – suspended
development – that when things
get tough, you take a break.

You, the deadliest insect on Earth,
carrier of disease, killer
of one million people each year.

Under a Moreton Bay fig
where kookaburras and seagulls
swooped to take the food
from our hands, your lethal embryos
could lie dormant for years
until conditions are ideal for hatching.

Can you hear that? He'd said that last night.
Are all the doors shut?
Then he'd reached
for the mosquito repellent.

Now I pull the bedsheet over my head,
grateful for the silence
that follows his absence.

What Happened to the Sun

We took that hot ball of glowing gases
at the heart of our solar system for granted,
so much intense energy and heat
bearing down on green city spaces
when she went out to walk the dog,
winter warmth brightening her face. Sometimes
under a large red gum she stopped
to watch a mother and son
play cricket or an elderly tennis player
limp towards the courts, 'No running
today, eh?' calls out his opponent. 'I'll keep
the ball on your forehand.'
Difficult to stay upbeat sometimes
when you see so much change. You
wish for things to be how they were before,
nourished by moon on water,
first stars, mountains, ocean,
a dog pulling on a lead under a bright sky,
beneath a cache of clouds,
wanting the time before,
before polar bears were in danger,
when, ignorantly, you basted your skin
in coconut oil on the hot sand,
before we were all bound by rules,
distanced in unusual ways
burning in the sun side by side
on a crowded beach.

Oksana

'The seaside should definitely be beneficial
when it comes to respiratory or skin allergies,'
a dermatologist reported.

During the pandemic a newspaper story warned:
*When Oksana started using hand sanitiser at the beach
she nearly died.*

Before the pandemic Oksana had perfect
lily-white smooth skin
but sitting on a park bench
or touching merchandise sprayed
with disinfectant made her body burn.

*It started on my hands, progressed up my arms,
my torso and my legs, she said. One day
it spread all over my face.*

Her skin fell off and then she lost her hair.
Oksana says she's lucky to be alive. A new drug
for allergic diseases made her better
but will she get back to the beach one day?

Reading about her recovery was a relief.
But it wasn't a relief to read that rising house prices
near the beaches during lockdown cost up to four
times the city average.

The great Australian dream of surf, sand and sun –
But can ocean breezes blow allergens away?
Not for Oksana.

This is the saddest line in the story.

The Invasion

Mulchers, Stump Grinders, Arborists,
lining up, a military mobilisation
called in for the massacre.
We jogged down the hill
as a feeble sun stayed hidden.

'It's an invasion,' my running buddy says.

We squeezed past the team in protective jackets
waiting near their vehicles drinking coffee,
checking phones, puffing on a last smoke,
lined up for the slaying along the road's corridor,
silhouetted against an ashen sky.

'Watch out!' the front-runner yells. 'Car coming.'

and an SUV belches up the hill
and forces us to withdraw to the footpath,
occupies the narrow road
as thunder ruptured the air.

A sea of purple bell-shaped jacaranda
scattered below our feet,
a carpet of slimy blossoms,
wedging themselves between
the ripples of our soles to take us down,
as the wind blustered more fallen flowers
and dead leaves beneath us.

And then the rain came down –

It stopped our whingeing,
just advanced us down the hill towards home
as crows and ravens shrieked overhead
into the gunmetal grey sky.
Birds, not bombs.

It took three days for next door's
strong, verdant tree,
standing alone for more than a hundred years,
to be gouged, hacked apart and removed.
When I looked out my window and saw what was gone,
what wasn't there, saw the bare,
mutilated tree stump, I mourned.

But it was the season of sunshine and gratitude.
It was the season of wondering what we'd do
if there were bombs in our sky instead of birds,
winters without electricity,
who would we be forced to become?

'Don't you feel isolated in Australia?'
'No,' I said. 'It's safe. And warm.'

East Coast Low

The rain bomb took its time forcing
its way down the coast towards us.
The dangerous winds waited in the wings.
Would our old house survive the onslaught?

We'd seen pictures of overflowing dams,
flash flooding, people trapped in ceilings
and on roofs waiting to be rescued,
cattle herds swept away along rivers,
washing up on beaches.

When the downpour hit us
it crippled the city, torturing roads into rivers,
public transport chaos, and soured
Sydney Harbour a murky brown.

Stories of exploding mosquito numbers,
snakes & spiders, leeches & rodents.

We ready ourselves for invasion.

Outside, a drowned rat swings
from the beak of a kookaburra.
Other birds queue on the clothes line
ready to plummet in attack.

Imagination

The creative is the place where no one else has ever been.
You have to leave the city of your comfort and go into the
wilderness of your intuition.

–Alan Alda

Buoyancy

How does poetry soothe me, I wonder.
Because it warms like hot chocolate.
I can drink it in and float on the words
that comfort and nourish.

I struggle against the pull of flood waters
and poetry cadences become a rescue dinghy.
I remember the day I was engulfed by words
all the way along the floor of the valley.
People were celebrating
after the storms and floods
while I struggled to climb out of the ravine
on the rain-sullied track I used to love.

Suddenly, I found the buoyancy of poetry,
its pulses hauling me up.
Poems as transporters, miracles,
not Moses parting the Red Sea kind,
but warmth of the sun after
days of rain offering hope.
I wanted to pause and absorb the brightness,
but I kept climbing, thinking,
'This is the way I need to proceed,'
then praying that it was.

First Words

Some days the words stay out of reach,
ships that have left the dock.
We don't get to climb aboard,
now we're scratching around,
watching, listening,
pointing a lens at anything
that moves or makes a noise.

The autumn leaves gather,
leaving a backwash
on damp asphalt:
CATCH ME IF YOU CAN.
I'm looking for patterns,
a spiky palm frond between
terracotta houses
anything to glimpse
that fires my mind.

Then, beside me in the café,
words fall in the air.
All at sea, I hear:
outsourcing
universal messaging
intrinsic motivation
landing page

Is this the snatch of dialogue
that will take hold
and not let go?

From Time to Time

My fountain pen glides
like a surfer riding a roll
a cutback in one fluid move

My desk looks refreshed
perhaps I dusted it
moved the papers to the other side
of the room

Mini-changes
alter spaces

Rotating fan
on a window ledge packed away
ballpoint pens on standby
in a clay mug

I puzzle over placement of small things
A motif?
Hand quickening
Morning shadows mark the tiles

Weavers

A well-hidden spider
created patterns
outside my office window
against the wooden frame.
I'd see the new progression
of her magnum opus
from my writing desk.
I'd be weaving plot entanglements
and she'd have shown off
her vision
to fast-moving days
as the year raced to its ending.
In the afternoons I'd be outside
hanging washing
picking up broken branches
watering herbs
and she'd have converted
moths and small flies into
sticky brown blobs.
A kookaburra laughed
from the clothes line.
Daily spider prompts helped drive me,
our compulsions to create on either
side of the glass.
One day the cleaner
sprayed the windows,
splattered and splashed,
with his power-hose.
By noon all surfaces
shone brightly.

Did the spider live?
Did she find a different hideout?
Her masterpiece is imprinted
on my brain:
its scaffolding
beginnings,
endings.

Legacy

It seemed both proper and at the same time deeply unfair
that so much of life was left to chance.
– Claire Keegan

Regrets

Driving through the streets of the city
on a Sunday, we're talking about
our crazy mistakes, the men we separated from,
the ex-husbands who remarried and married again,
those we shouldn't have let go.
'Yes, it's hard having no one to turn to,' you say,
reversing into a 'no stopping' space.
The signpost doesn't mention Sundays.
You turn the ignition off
and cover your face with your hands.
'I'm so hopeless at parking,' you cry. 'He used to tell me
we'd need to catch a cab to the kerb.'
I laugh and pat your shoulder.
'It's fine,' I say. 'You're sticking out a bit in front,
but you can try again…or not. Nothing's perfect.'
My words surprise me,
rising above the rush of traffic,
a sweet fortune cookie prediction,
forgive yourself,
you did your best.

Attached

I've made so many foolish decisions
you'd think I'd tread differently.

In winter
empty skies turn cobalt blue.
A myna bird steps across
a table top
and the whole café is on alert.
Is that the bird's scat
on my chair,
or a small brown twig?

Take care. Don't brush
strange things away
with your sleeve like I did.

Here the cut gerberas droop.
Who will sever the softened stems
now that you have gone?

I remember the afternoons
we walked through the cemetery
memorising names on headstones,
painful stories from our childhoods
opening us to tenderness.

So many days have passed now,
but here I am still,
stuck at the end of the road.

A Cup of Moments

Nights that nourish like slow-cooked meat
a gremolata on top or not, plenty to eat no matter
how many are home.
A side of mashed potato and peas, a ladle
ready for seconds. Maybe a baguette of garlic bread
divided into slices. I like setting out the plates & cutlery
on the bench-top, the way you come home
on those nights you know I'll be here. I am happy
when you help yourself to more without asking.

When you were eight, we built Lego cars
that hurtled over ramps, you laughed
when they splashed into tubs
of water. And I remember exactly that day
you said you'd go to see
the boy down the road instead.

A friend consoled me: 'If he'd preferred
staying home playing games
with his grandma, I'd be worried.'
Now, when my daughter warns, 'Be careful
not to ask him too many questions –
got it?'

I clutch the cup of slow-simmering moments,
keeping a tight lid on it all
making sure nothing catches or burns.

The Dark

I'll open the door to you, broad blade
that divides my dreams.
I'll count your many carriages,
your clanking wheels.

What exactly did you want
all these years? That young girl
never made it out, that sunny one.
Only the catastrophiser made it through.

On the run, out west
I felt strung up
hanging by my laces.
In the murky gloom I was tied to you
for a whole week of despair.

You were waiting for me down south,
up north, and on the coast,
drugged by the sea's remote horizon
guarded by my huge straw hat.

Enough! It's enough!
See the doona falling
to the floor.
It's hard to stay in the dark here
where the tree canopy protects
with its attention-grabbing beauty,
and we could stop there
and never face backwards again.

Breaking Out

See that white terrace house?
You could live in the attic there.
Yes, I like an eyrie, looking
out on the world. I wanted to be locked
in a tower, a princess in a fairy tale,
when I was a child.
I'm still the girl dreaming of breaking out.
Maybe she's learnt to abseil now.
Some terraces have small colourful gardens
at the front. I prefer fragrant cut flowers
in a vase. I belong to
that discreet sect of law-breakers
who snip buds over a fence. A close escape
gives me an adrenalin kick.

Reconstruction

What the Russians have destroyed can readily be replaced with the latest, most modern, green and digital infrastructure. – President Zelenskyy

We used to knit and sew and crochet,
to fold paper aeroplanes,
and make bubble-blowers out of paper clips.
Enough of the doom and gloom.
Let's construct a different world.

When my sister was a child,
and sent to live in a convent,
her only toys were empty match boxes.
So she built doll's house furniture.
She brought her tiny innovations home
in school holidays to show me.
And that's how she became
the designing woman she is to this day.

Bewildered

When I was four
I asked my big brother
Is Mum the wicked
queen from Snow White?

He fell about with laugher,
then wrestled me to the ground
using his knees to pin
my shoulders to the floor.

My brother, the bully.
But I loved him.

Years later, when our mother said she
had heart problems, my brother told her
it was impossible.
How can you? he said.
You don't have a heart.

The questions still disturb me to this day.

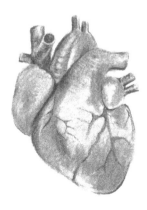

When the New Boyfriend Nearly Died

In the hospital's public toilet, your face pleads back at you, white and worried. Far as you know, your new boyfriend had a heart attack while bouncing between your child-bearing hips. Too much of a strain. It's not your fault. When he was admitted to Emergency you didn't know if you'd ever see him again.

After five hours of waiting, you ask the receptionist if you can go in. When she asks you, you can't pronounce his Polish surname. You spell out the letters. She considers you through the gap in the partition. You tell her you're his new girlfriend. *So you're the one*, she must be thinking before pressing the red button that lets you in.

He is lying in bed, a canula in his arm. His eyes are closed. You sit in a chair beside him and hold his hand. This would never have happened if it weren't for you. Nurses and doctors hurry past clutching clipboards.

Don't die on me, you plead.

If he dies, what you will miss are his text messages of love, the thwack of his body, and the pots of Japanese tea you shared. In bed you'd sip from tiny ceramic mugs.

You make a mental list of your strengths and weaknesses: you're good at hedonistic pleasures, bad at cryptics, bad at lonely Sundays, good at making new friends, bad at staying in touch, good at making loose-leaf tea after sex with an addict, good at falling for men who can't stop swallowing uppers and downers. Good at loving your new boyfriend who took too many pills and now you're worried he'll die.

Are you dreaming, or did he just squeeze your hand?

Country

Nature never did betray
The heart that loved her.
– William Wordsworth

Crows Never Forget

       can we remember like they do
through long rain-drenched months
       with their clever chat?
one warns the others   a human who scared them
years ago   but the crows when the sky cleared
       cried out loud and raucous
near the top-floor balcony
       trellised with spring buds
crow-speech channelling new connections into
       the sides of my head

On the Path

It's green out here.

There are cliffs with straight up-and-down faces,
high-rise breeding havens for mud nesters.

I'm wanting to know
what the birds have to teach us,
but their calls are intermittent,
faint and repetitive, shrill and squawking.

I gaze over the cliffs and across the valley,
a sacred mountain range turned blue
by forests of eucalyptus, where tourists
of every colour crowd the lookouts.
Are they seeking spiritual wisdom
from the mighty mountains?

I would like to know how a lyrebird
learns its complex songs,
or how to laugh heartily like a kookaburra.
We could find vantage points
above daisies and banksias,
butterflies and mountain devils.

On this bush track – the signposted path
to a waterfall – down steps made of logs,
a man stops unexpectedly in front of me.
He squeezes and inhales the leaf of a tea tree.
I too am a believer in the healing power
of plants and in mythical mountains
and holy pilgrimages.

A majestic wedge-tailed eagle
whistles a soft peal
before soaring above us.

The sound of the waterfall
draws me onward.

Circle of Life

In a pond below the waterfall,
on the day of the nearly-one-hundred-
year-old Queen's funeral,
after her 70-year-and-214-day reign,
a freshwater turtle basks on a rock.

Are his eyes open or closed?

The turtle's curious neck scans
the weeds for aquatic insects – he's
nearly one hundred too and revered
by indigenous communities. Speckled
long-fin eels lurk in the muddy
bottom of the stream.

How can these shape-shifting, slippery
fish push their way inland from
their place of birth in the sea,
slithering over land, climbing waterfalls,
taking down serious prey – all without legs?

Will they reach one hundred too before
their final swim – the epic journey,
thousands of kilometres – a return
to the deep ocean to die?

And what will they be remembered for?

The centenarian turtle unfolds
his lower lids and blinks,
then withdraws beneath
his crusty shell.

Black Birds

In leafy trees.
Are they crows or ravens up there,
the bases of their feathers
crow-white, or raven-grey?
Is it true crows can recognise people
who befriend them for years after?
Alert, *National Wildlife* warns,
crows stop and watch you
rather than you watch them.
Fly away, birds, to wide open spaces,
find an anthill, let the ants climb on,
rub them into your black feathers, for
another day of blitzing aggressors –
Aren't you afraid they'll swoop? I ask
my friend who likes to walk
beneath their roosting sites.
She smiles, 'They're crows. They know
a pal when they see one.'

Away

We stop in the Blue Mountains above
the sandstone escarpment at Govetts Leap.
All day the wilderness opens in our heads,
a larger story. We keep watch, staring across
gaping canyons, imagine ourselves restored
beneath the giant waterfalls.

A young man using a rain
umbrella to protect himself from the heat,
It will cool down at night –
I could stay longer, till the white
mountain mist cancels out the sun.

At Echo Point we look out to the unusual
rock formation, the Three Sisters.
Aboriginal Dreaming legend says
three sisters were turned to stone.

I close my eyes to hear the stories
told around campfires since the beginning of time.
Don't leave this place of artistic genesis,
ancient rock carvings, handprints on cave walls.

Tell me this mountain range – ravaged
at times by mountain fire – won't change;
the wonder will keep opening our eyes
to the 100 species of eucalypts,
400 animal species,
lush, or rugged, or opaque –
blue haze scattered by the sun,
listening to its inarticulate silence.

Acknowledgements

Some of the poems in this collection were first published in the following journals and anthologies:

Quadrant – 'When the New Boyfriend Nearly Died', 'Regrets', 'Words', 'Transience', 'When Will It End', 'On the Path', 'Electioneering On the Mall', 'Crows Never Forget', 'Flat White, One Sugar', 'What Could We Say', 'Weavers', 'Tactics', 'Bewildered', 'What Happened To the Sun', 'A Refuge';

Burrow, Old Water Rat Publishing – 'Holding On';

Poems & Prose by Women of the World for Ukraine – 'Twisted Tea';

Canberra Times Panorama Arts Section – 'Jogger At My Heels' and 'Breaking Out'.

Milton Keynes UK
Ingram Content Group UK Ltd.
UKHW030017010324
438562UK00014B/379